Unfinished Building

Unfinished Building

POEMS BY TOBY OLSON

COFFEE HOUSE PRESS :: MINNEAPOLIS :: 1993

Of the poems in this volume, the following have been published in limited editions: "Patterns" appeared as "Messing Around With Patterns: English & American" in the Perishable Press book *Doctor Miriam;* "Gulls," "Faces," "Moot," and "Some Small Movements" are from the Perishable Press book *Birdsongs;* "Gulls" also appeared in the Membrane Press book *Home.*

"Faces" and "Moot," together with two other Birdsongs, have been set for voice and piano by the composer Paul Epstein and first performed in 1988 in Philadelphia.

Some of the poems here appeared (at times in slightly different versions) in the following magazines, to which grateful acknowledgment is made: *Anima, Atlantic Review, Boundary 2, Conjunctions, The Friendly Local Press, Gegenschein Quarterly, Mulch, New Directions in Prose and Poetry, New Letters, Ninth Decade* (London), *#, Occurrence, The Paris Review,* and *Temblor.*

The publishers would like to thank the following funders for assistance which helped make this book possible: the Bush Foundation; the Dayton Hudson Foundation on behalf of Dayton's and Target Stores; The General Mills Foundation; The Lannan Foundation; The McKnight Foundation; The Andrew W. Mellon Foundation; The National Endowment for the Arts, a federal agency; The Beverly J. and John A. Rollwagen Fund of the Minneapolis Foundation; and Star and Tribune/Cowles Media Company. Major new marketing initiatives have been made possible by the Lila Wallace-Reader's Digest Literary Publisher's Marketing Development Program, funded through a grant to the Council of Literary Magazine and Presses.

This activity is made possible in part by a grant provided by the Minnesota State Arts Board, through an appropriation by the Minnesota State Legislature.

Coffee House Press books are available to the trade through our primary distributor, Consortium Book Sales & Distribution, 1045 Westgate Drive, Saint Paul, MN 55114. For personal orders, catalogs or other information, write to : Coffee House Press, 27 North Fourth Street, Suite 400 Minneapolis, MN 55401

Library of Congress Cataloging in Publication Data
   Unfinished building : poems / by Toby Olson.
      p.   cm.
   ISBN 1-56689-009-8
   1. Title.
   PS3565.L84U5   1993
      811'.54—dc20   93-15299, CIP
9, 8, 7, 6, 5, 4, 3, 2, 1

Contents

Always,

for Miriam

Rose Poem

Seeing the yellow roses along the fence
  and the honeysuckle
  and that around each separate cluster
          weeds have grown that are
  particular to each and hold
  tight against, but under
  those
        strange guarding umbrellas
  of yellow buds and leaves—

I think
  the weeds may be more
  complex still than are the roses:
  the way they change each year
  in color, size and form, and shift
  their attitudes around the yard.

And what of the human sense in which
  we usually see these aspects
          —though truly of another world
  that we need guarding too
  and succoring, as if
  our frail loves
  were the aura of an awning placed
  against the sun, and the ones
  we hold against
  were stronger than ourselves?

These roses (truly
       of another world) are sometimes
choked off from their own sustenance
and the weeds, thick and ugly when compared to them
and the honeysuckle, take over—
but there is very little left to take
when beauty dies.

And so my love come back again
into some suffering
some pleasure and some resolve;
         the weeds are no less tender
in their need
even if they tend to overdo it a bit
they grow more strong and complex still
close to the honeysuckle
and the rose.

American Scat

The crippled cat next door
  with his broken and paralyzed leg
      comes sideways and crablike across the yard
though in a straight line with obvious motive.

He's looking for my cat, who is
in most cases afraid of nothing,
chases
  dogs, people and cats out
usually, would bite a nail in half
were it offered,
  but in this case she yowls
and hides under the porch
trembling.

      The easy hypothesis
for such things: she is
faked out by the hanging paw, the foreign,
wounded and familiar
  (or is it projection?

I remember, in a friend's talk, a crippled beggar
with no legs and one arm
  coming at him in India,
him
giving him money, but holding back
for the others he knows he'll meet
later.

      The easy hypothesis:
a sense of guilt
  (about what though?

What if his money goes,
the insides of his pockets held out
  in his fingertips, and then his clothes,
and maybe he cuts his legs off too, gets
a board with wheels,
            and then
gets beat out of his due
maybe killed by the skill
and mastery of the other
man holding his palm out at crotch level
now—
  better to drop a coin into it,
you can't win.

    Ah, my friends
    it takes more days than we've got
    to get things finally
    together, to keep loose and yet
            move on to our demise:

the cows low and walk together in the fields,
possessed of a certain style they go
full up with milk, so
single-minded it seems
  that the field itself
is moving: the way sky moves like a film
when sparrows flock,
the way the ice cap moves
quite literally
  around the pole— ghost herds,
and we, the riders go
together, in correct order
in our dreams.

Old broken paw limps in the rolled-in fog
back, into his own yard.
          It's very foggy here;
it's been that way, with rain, for ten days almost,
and that's why I think of Mexico:

first time there, to meet a friend, I sat
in a bar in Tijuana waiting, when a little man
came down the row of stools with a little box
with handles, stopped
   to negotiate here and there
and when he reached my place,
said —very directly—"Wanna buy an electric shock?"
What could I say, but
                    "How much?"
"A quarter," he said and offered the handles.
It wasn't bad at all.

          The easy hypothesis:
private enterprise,
work, and a sense of dignity,
but *my God!* electric shocks?

 (though it does clear the fog a little.

 The rich get rich, and the poor get
 the by-products and the waste
    of riches, never
 get the rich themselves
 but the myth only
 that the rich are also
 poor—
          after all
 what have they got

but riches?
   and magic stomachs
   and golden hemorrhoids
   and Lucite toilet seats
   and silent plumbing.

The fog is completely gone now, and I find
I have completely surrounded myself
with bird feeders:
grackles come, the cowbirds, some
sparrows,
        nothing
I'd built them for really.
Loaded with thistle,
the ones for the beautiful birds
stand full and empty, maybe
too close to my window,
   to humankind
for them.

And then,
that in its turn gives thought too
   to all those birds in Washington:
the Mad Parliament
of Foul Play in America
emerging always as a standard of excellence:

   what did you think Mad Martha was talking about,
madness?

        The bigger birds
push out the small. The sparrows are agile though
and very persistent, and when
the grackles come

too close to their nests,
they drive them out in pairs—

that's an American Nature Metaphor
and irrelevant—

    it's the starlings we've got to worry about:
    the false eggs.

        O,
      come and live with me
      ye little birds, and bring me more
      than foolish and dull pain
      for a public joy.

Fun in the country.
Fun in *our* Country.

America,
      sweetheart, you mad devil,
what have you wrought or engendered here?
It seems
   it's gotten into the grain of the wood itself
   I've made these feeders from
and the grain I feed:

thistle
cracked corn
wild bird seed:

Nixon
    Reagan
        Bush,

or anyone in that order,
foreign, wounded and familiar.
Each, in his own way
makes hay,
            and there
all birds in common feed
without rancor.

        The easy hypothesis?—
the cat comes again,
the rising sphinx or avenging angel,
and wipes them all out
fairly.

    It is a dream
of justice only
like all metaphor,
a correct world
in which
        the quality of judgment
is constrained
by conscience
we all have
    or would
if the world were straight,
but it isn't.

The real birds hassle each other,
the big ones kick
    the little ones off the feeder—
the catbirds sing—
    the sparrows double up and chase
the grackles off—

        the starlings
        lay false eggs—
the red-winged blackbird
is mindless, but very tough,
the cat hides
under the porch and shudders still
in the memory of that odd and pathetic gesture.

All living things in chaos gather.

And up
in a realm like morals above
        these small and subtle shifts of feeling,
hawks and gulls and eagles move
and finally
            Sky Labs, Ghost Riders, and the free satellites.

And then
that final reversal
in which we too are held,
        captive,
earthbound,
in dreams of Justice and Right Action,
relative, minuscule and passing,
in ghost herds.

Come,
let us go now, you and I
even into the bathroom together—

the great leveler, the place
of primary movements
and old jokes,

like the one about cows
sent up into space:

the herd shot round the world—

    a final and sound hypothesis:
a twisted history,
a flat dimension.

And when we lift the seat it reads
American Standard
or Mad Cliff.

Clouds

for P.B.

The cold cereal turns to mush in the bowl
and the rain comes again, only
a few drops at first
on the upright pane.
        the windows open and flanking
already run; sand spots widen on the central glass.
the cereal
tastes good: blueberries and sliced banana
and raisins ride on the mush.
                            and at this moment
I can imagine nothing that would not bring pleasure
times even when indigestion is a welcome occurrence,
it stirs the body.
                wind now
and complete void of ideas, imagination, craft
of texture.
            mush in the bowl,
maybe the fruit falls in a certain way
in which one could find some significance
were the search on.

There is fruit
but no leaves blowing. in the wind, the pane
on the left half dry, from the sun
now, which is open again

burning the fog off. the sky's
revealed in its magnitudes,

these clouds.

But look again, and down
It's not quite clear
but already there's a full meeting of the parliament
        tho, given cat and hawk,
it's a house of cards.

jackdaws, sparrows, blackbirds,
even the mournful doves sit
        on the boards and take feed,
and that too is mush
after the rain
we've had and continue
to have.

        the clouds break
into patterns, possible
named shapes. there's enuf
blue to make a pair of pants now:
it'll soon clear.
                the sky's
like an outdoor movie, in rain; wet shapes
just barely glimpsed on the screen, in a finger bowl,
continue to pass.

And what seems needful here is a sense of direction
How else talk about clouds? Methinks, I see
what could be a burden to an empty mind:
        dark, bedroom lace at the edge of shapes
        changing
        like some dramatic shawl:

all
we need is love of
what is here before us
close to ground—

that may be so, but
I can hear hounds running
across these foggy moors
  in the middle of all this truth
(a likely story.

The cereal is
almost completely melted now.
      the fruit begins to turn, and falls
in patterns from the rim.
                              the clouds
begin to cook and turn
to misty fog above the bay. I count
six drops of driving rain against the pane.

      *

It feels like a little flower, she said
      (Anaïs Nin? de Beauvoir?)
I was alive that time.

You'd read it somewhere:
like a soft & magic flower pressed
against your thigh.
      I felt that way,

not like a bud that opens.
   one that's done
      past prime & close to death;
magic
is that it opens again:
      stamen & two tight buds.

The sparrows, huddled
under the feeder's roof in fog.
    It is not odd to find, in winter
    40 sparrows in a martin house
    pressed together for warmth.
I do not press
or leave a handprint on the pane.
I count the bits of fruit in pairs to give me words.
    As a cloud of anger or sadness
    follows the man indoors in a comic strip,
there is no way to name this matrix or these forms.

        *

I'm dead some years agone, the 13th day
next month. I might have said it that way
agone,
        and rhymed with something odd
and yet completely expected,
maybe *wan,*
so we could feel
the thought was all our own,
could sing primarily just the same
as me
    (at least with the same joy.
My gulls float, then turn away
in fog
and with them goes
whatever compromised thoughts are held.
A song is a game of Spell against Ideas,
a drink of prune juice upon rising.
Values
are left to silence

unless they sing.
A man sits and copies the birds' songs in the fog.
He does it because his tongue
can try to move that way.
    That is enuf of reason.
Hello, pulse.

        *

But look again, and down;
a small breeze rises here,
 pushing drops on the pane,
opening holes in the fog.

 our doves
with beaks held high
walk around in the mist.
                    the ground
in smoke, reminds me of Brigadoon (the hounds help
the image) and I'm
speaking of warped love again:

that way
I make you move here
much like a foggy mirror,
every turn,
each strut I'd put you through,
    It's not your self I'm praising.

Could I spread
your body on that anvil I protest
is love of you, I know
that it would happen
somewhere else,

outside this room,
this place that now becomes
      so bright within its animal darkness
      it could burn the tissues.
All our wives are gathered
in a fog,
and Christ! I can imagine such
      clarity of purpose from that vantage,
I am left apart from them
because of words.
                        I see
the birds are climbing
once again. I cannot hold them to their names.
The changing fog is patchy. I remember
in a fog they set the dogs on me
      to bite my legs and ankles in Vermont.
I had a mother once.
I was alive that time.
It was
more various than that.

      *

I lived a portion of my life—that part
before its end—in a sickroom
counting birds.
                  My son would come
so shyly to my bed. I couldn't eat hard food.
The window at my foot, its beveled edge imagined
mirror of a possible life
in which my son would pass
daily.

I had a sense of humor once.
Everything brought pleasure:
indigestion, sound of my son's
foot on the porch,
mush in a bowl,
        the count of birds.

and now

my terms come in a sudden rush:
it is a love of death & sickness he beholds

is what he is: an empty chest, a vessel
ready to be filled. I cannot speak

the vowels of our names aloud. I cannot
help but want to kiss & touch

the growth of clustered cherries upon your breast.
Each one was strange & beautiful in their death.

And in the morgue they'd wake him up
so he could count their marks and scars.

I was alive those times.

        *

It begins
        to come down
more certain than before:
a spotty rain you find
very much like blood between your legs:

the flower
petals spot and sag with dew, the evidence
of a femininity that sometimes burns,
the way drops do in a sudden rain upon
a sunburned arm
        above a cast,
a spotted napkin
shriveling into parchment in the sun;

comes down again
in a crazy cycle we can't read
although we apprehend
configuration of its form,
its certainty. The birds seem
momentarily frantic in its wash, that
        rise and fall,
that shuddering in the wings
to set them right, and after a moment
stand again, resigned
and careful where they are. the window
fogs again and then it melts
its steam.

        *

I left a piece of my forehead in San Francisco
and the good use of both legs in Vermont.
My right knee lost its mobility in Ohio
and I cashed in three feet of intestine in Arizona.

The skin of my teeth left me for a woman in Bisbee
and my faith went sour in Corpus Christi.
Bowels' juice drained out with fat in Los Angeles
and my right arm fell apart in Colorado.

There are wet shirts, hung
like sick skin
        over clotheslines in Hollywood,
my father's body strung like bedroom lace
in a walnut tree, in El Monte.
Hounds
I have owned still sniff in the shrubs
whining against property.

Tucson,
mother and I
asleep in the hospital parking lot
near sunrise.

        Inside
they are ripping my father open,
drop
pieces of mesentery into a bucket.

'You could have slept *here*
in a hospital bed,'
the nurses said.

The motels thought I was my mother's lover;
we couldn't get in.

I was 14.

Pissing in the empty lot, I watched them
empty buckets of flesh and blood in a trash bin.

We were alive that time.

I was holding
myself like a healthy flower
under the slate clouds of morning.

    *

My dears,

I write against the chance

you might construe the fact

these clouds will dissipate

as evidence

    of a lack of constancy:

the quiet

certain nature of our love, our lives,

the way

    you press and touch

and cure the very skin on me,

daily.

    Even though

the sickness always comes again,

and stronger,

        all my women

kept my breaking life together.

It was more various than that:

I was alive that time.

Each one had the very flower of me.

I could not die

    until I died,

for living.

Faces

Inch by inch
the rain comes in off the bay
   rolls in in a changing cloud
folds of the cloud's face,
ripples of brow
             crosses
   the acres of space between
  my face in a window
the bay's submerged profile.

someone
is maybe walking the bay's beach now
unseen, where it may
     be clear, watching
the newly revealed clarity of blue
sky above it. there
may be birds there.

2 faces . one able
only to see thru a 3rd face in the glass now
beyond where, what
     elegant figure walks on the beach?

   it is myself
   it is an old friend
   it is some past
      lover in her perfection, is
   noone I know or remember
   has nothing to do with me
      is maybe not there at all. that may
   be its elegance.

dissolved & broken
the cloud forms into fog
                    into wet air
finally
the bay's beach reveals itself
subtly, changed in its shift of sand

There is no one there.

the fog closes again
my face in the window
rain on the pain.

Unfinished Building

The sun brings forth
false caroling from the trees—the old fool;
a season in transition. And the other fools
        climb to the roof again:
a single shingle, butted in, left flapping
lightly in the breeze,
      where they quit it
when the old fool was gone
and there was a hint of rain.

He shines again,
sending perverted messages to the birds,
      whose songs are tentative—
wiser than he is, closer to the earth.
Only a solitary cloud, but a sheet of haze,
and close (and just over the lip)
thicker ones, and rain again.

It's the fitful start of summer
close to the finish of June.
A stiff wind rises,
      blowing petals among the roses;
their own futures in their sight now—
a symmetry around a center
which is dying.

It was a dark and stormy night;
a band of robbers were sitting around a camp fire.
The leader spoke, "*Jack* tells a story!"
and Jack began:

"It was a dark and fitful night;
  a ring of robbers were sitting
around the ring of a camp fire. The leader spoke,
'Jack, tell us a story,' and Jack began"—

    It was the hour (before rain) of a false sun;
a jagged link of workmen
were sitting around a pile of shingles
on a new roof. One of them spoke out,
            into the breeze—
torn pages from a book—
a bright voice, indistinct, and laughter
    (shingles rising from the pile
and shifting, the wind stiffening);
tell us some sort of story,
of prefabricated houses
before it rains;
of nail guns, a power saw, the way the rafters
are jacked up by a crane,
    the house rising
in a single day, and Jack began:

"It was a tedious night of group therapy in Boston;
no propriety for cocaine, but the marijuana
    (oil, thick in our hair) perverted us to insight.
We were a group of fabricated thinkers,
sitting in a ring around a table
aflame with roses; some had
    buds in their hair. I was hooked in,
wired in, to thoughts about building:
everything
on center, each stud,
and flashing in the cheeks . . ."

I gathered the torn pages from the air,
and they were scrambling
down from the peak, and it was raining.

The rain wets the petals, a few
cling to the split rail;
        the pink and devastated roses
rise along the post:
a symmetry
around a center, which is dying.

It was a clear and lazy day in Savannah—
up North it was raining.
A band of casual acquaintances
        were gathered around each other, walking.
There was a fleamarket:
        old tools, glass roses and flashing.
Moss hung in the small parks,
Spanish restaurants, awkward in their architecture.
Somebody told a quick story,
soon forgotten.

Then came upon the house shell
and entered it.
        It had once been three stories;
and could see the notches in the brick,
rhythmic, and rising
where the beams had been set.
        There were trees dancing,
waving, in the empty frames, shifting shadows.
All the notches were perfect, true
and symmetrical
to the high ceiling.

Up North it was raining, water bleeding
along shingles
in the cheeks of false chimneys.
I lifted
the assembled book and smelled the pages.

But the roses! I was listening
to Bird across the water from Boston.
   It was a dark and stormy night,
but the band held
the station
               (a camp fire in the hearth).
I had salvaged two buds and a firecracker
honeysuckle more dramatic,
and one full bloom—already
pink petals
gathered around the small blue vase;

      Bird on the water, stormy
on a stormy night:
the dead sing better than the living.

The old fool is out again.
      The birds are unconvinced; only
a young sparrow tests him
swelling, on pine's limb, and facing him.

The young fools
stand at the flimsy walls (the sheets of mock cedar)
testing the breeze, turning in a small band,
laughing and joking.
      As the breeze shifts, from bay to backside,
I can hear them. One reaches for a headband

and adjusts it (a sweat or rain band):
I can make nothing out.

It was a dark and stormy night.
A band of arsonists were sitting around a camp fire
    in a cozy house shell in Savannah.
the leader spoke, *"Jack,* feed the fire."
And Jack began.

        The studs were thin kindling, the beams,
bowed from the span,
were cracked against his knee;
he crushed chunks of subflooring in his hands.
The leader spoke, picking his teeth
    with a post, "Jack, tell us a story!"
And Jack began.

        "It was summer, and the wild
wood was bleeding;
        amber of pine sap,
dark shadows of tree cutters in the forest.
One of them carried the work-load chit—
anything would do:
they could grind and press it,
call it board. The sun's
            branch-cut beams
lay in patterns on the sticky bark,
then faded: a storm was coming.
        (Down South it was mild and sunny.)
And they killed a tree
and built a smoky camp fire
from the raw wood."

But the roses! The dark
        and sweet smell of the fallen petals!
To keep the fool off,
I wet and stick one on my nose.
Thorns hold out stronger than standard nails;
a line of red sap, oozing
along my arm.

The birds are singing, the pines
full now,
a band of sparrows
in crooked chain on a thin limb.
            Dull thunk of the nail gun;
they're up on the roof again.

  I had imagined rain.
  I had imagined the moon setting
              the needle on center again,
  unwavering, the day moon—
  the sun brash and inconstant—
        the birds answering only to the moon,
  even the night birds
  in the day light.

        I had imagined Savannah—
  the house shell—my brother, Jack
  in Wisconsin,
        mild and sunny down South,
  a dark storm in the North:
  a dead player, but a live saxophone
  across the water.

I had been thinking about roses;
the way the house
        rose in the distance,
petals, and rows of sparrows.

Jack rows to the center
        of the flat mountain lake;
the bird is an osprey,
his voice screams on the water; he reconstructs
a crane in a bare tree;
        the crane is screaming, the tree shaking,
but the crane's house holds,
shudders, and holds.
                "Jack, tell us a story!"

And Jack began with a storm,
        fishing in high country
miles in.
It was crisp and clear, a blue sky,
        and rose at the tree tips like fire.
He was intent on the water,
until the water darkened: a sudden rain,
and then thunder and more rain,
and the trail flooded.

It rained for two days;
        there was a constant and stiff wind.
He built a lean-to against trees
in the rain, managed a small camp fire,
and stayed dry.

When the rain stopped, he came out.
It was a dark and stormy night,
        but there was a full moon.

He found he had built his house
against a tree
in which there was the tight, dry house
of an osprey.
That was the story.

Underneath this story:
        It was a bright night of remembrance in Boston
which is recorded, like therapy
in pages gathered—as if petals—into a book.
                Maybe it was not that:
Savannah? Wisconsin? a saxophone?

It could have been
a band of children sitting around a camp fire—
Pepperdine, the Boy Scouts, 1947—
        twisting plastic strands
into lanyards: everyone to have a whistle
for warning, keeping the household ghosts off,
possible tent fires.

The leader spoke, "Jack, tell us a ghost story,"
but Jack was missing.
We found him
snug, in the log house,
writing.

        And for punishment:
to build a small cabin with Lincoln Logs,
to true up each angle,
doorway and frame. In a window,
on a small chair, he put a saxophone;
        there were shingles, a stoop,
a stone chimney—

a wonder of ingenuity—
emblem of the country: tight fitted notches.

And the leader stood
straight on the caps at the peak, half mesmerized,
looking out the window and across the water
    (at Boston? Savannah? Wisconsin?);
the house held, and Jack began:

It was a dark and stormy night.
A band of robbers were sitting around a camp fire.
The leader spoke, "*Jack* tells a story!"
And Jack began—

    and the story unpeeled like a sheath
of onionskin paper, a book
made of pulp in Savannah, from wood cut
in Wisconsin, sold in Boston—
  of fine trees used to make saxophone reeds;
there was no moon, but band held bars
of Bird over the water
      the bright bay,
and over the Bird, dark clouds:
unexplainable rose petals on the bay's surface.

And the story continued to the first light of morning;
the clouds were clearing,
    and Jack began
bringing his head up: to discover
he was alone at a desk among scattered pages,
rectangular petals.
      The sky was vacant;
the old fool shone forth.

Out the window,
the roses were buttons on the stems.

And there, in the distance, the innocent house
had risen in the turn of one day—
        the band of young fools sat,
gathered around the false chimney at the peak;
they were laughing and telling stories.

        Their leader, the architect-builder,
was on the ground
standing among the discards,
hands on his hips, looking up, and smiling.

Jack could make out the songs of the sparrows,
the dead, alive in the saxophone, across the water.
        He saw the clouds
move in over the strains, saw the architect-
builder look up also.

Both Jack
and the leader knew
that before the day ended
it would be dark and stormy.

El Monte

In El Monte, the maniacs
ran on the dirt roads on their bicycles;
some carried the *Times,* even then
      the weight of wet rags
rolled into tubes: 50 or more
Sunday-onlys. Christ
   you're at it again
rolling before the first light,
in the smoke of smudge pots,
apparitional brains of orange trees, a maniac
in California.

Freedom forever:
no excuse this morning; it was sunny at 6,
    then the storm came on, completely visible—
a blanket of low-hung clouds,
black as smudging, a line in from the bay.
      Was your blanket pulled
back up over you, and were you sleeping again?
El Monte,
a force in the lives of many;
where are you, and do you remember?

     To be elegant and straight;
to stand up straight.
To be relevant, but not glorious, invisible,
not at odds.
  To stand straight up in a crowd,
going unnoticed, but to go in
for a job or a marriage—
to be hired, above all others because

you stand straight (the truss
        forcing your shoulders back,
until it becomes habit).

El Monte—
that a man close to 50 can remember you—
eucalyptus and berry vine;
    you're turning in your truss,
turning the white column of your neck, adolescent
assertiveness:
    small chin, small mounds in the mesh,
wide shoulder straps
        your back like a wide
white board,
the torch of your yellow hair.

It was a hell without music
hell, of the twists of adolescence seeping
        down into childhood—
did I hug my sister?
was my mouth in that hellish O?
You took your white shirt off to show us,
told us
        to stand up straight (I imagined
to avoid such torture):
freedom forever from the babysitter.

Bellows pushing the blanket to waves, or
under the waves,
    white dolphin in clear water,
sheet caps at the tips; or a burial—
waves of the wrapped body
        under the waves of the sea—
waves of memory, El Monte: probably

not where you are.
       But what do you think of (a woman of 60)
when you take pause, on a rainy day?
Probably not El Monte.
Think of anything— La Puente,
       a town on the outskirts, a trailer park,
the light
that is always wakefulness,
a musical chime of whitecaps on the bay,
the entire sea of memory.

              And thinking of you, it's a turbulence;
now I am too old for you—
still wanting you— this maniacal
pedaling fool.
Was it your father dressed you: white shirt
       and fake white pearls of his story,
a white skirt
to stand up straight in,
gave you money?
Who would live in El Monte
       (dirt roads and orange groves)
but the poor?

And you *did* stand straight,
       took freedom from your father's trappings,
stood behind twisted
              net of vines in eucalyptus;
stripped to your truss—
wide, animal straps at your shoulders—
       you turned for us,
pornographic beyond the consciousness
of young boys who watched you,

at a good distance, smoking the vines:
            the lift of your small breasts,
and turned for us,
who were empty of all thoughts of freedom,
our mouths in those hellish Os.

And later, it was said to be
La Puente—
        Mexicans in the trailer park
your truss hung on a nail
driven into a tree (I imagine
            free of the torture, a still
white harness in the moonlight).

And you are 60,
and I am still, at times, that maniac.
        I think I remember passing you, once
at 6 AM, in your white outfit;
you were heading home,
a weight of the *Times* on my handlebars.
It was cold, and they were smudging.

        And did you pause, obscurely, in the smoke
and watch me? And out of it
a tightening in my thighs, a thrust to erectness,
or have I made this up?

Your father is surely dead now.
        It's 6 AM, and you are sleeping;
here,
the bay rises up to whitecaps
in a breeze.

Why don't you wake up, wake up!

Freedom forever—
    we can go down from the mountain, El Monte,
from the twisted vines, and our memory,
into the valley
where all the trees are straight.

Floobie

Yesterday we got up early, or I did;
you stayed: the quiet
    slopes of your body still covered,
a little private talk.

And when you got up, I heard you
(was sanding in the basement) and was
        thrown for a minute—
what was that sound?
why is it
leaving a place or coming
things impinge in their quiet complexities
on us?

    (floobie)

You were tinkering around with the coffee;
  I was sanding
and heard the unspecifiable sound as *floobie*
and touched the objects I was working with
fresh again. why
in the bodies of concrete things, such identifications?
         the way
the paper becomes impacted slowly
as one is sanding;
  wood gives
    up under its roughness,
the burled grain, the paper
finally sliding easier,
pores of the hand loaded,
the job finished as the friction quits:

hand in wood
floobie
into *shoobie-do.*

Well, it was old times, the sound
was a piece of performance,
a friend's name
        before he was a friend
but was close to others
who are friends,

and I was sanding
the wood forward
floobie & backward *floobie-do.*

Armand, i.e.
scat-singer (but that was in another time
& life), now poet, translator, friend,
student, possible divorcee
        or fatherless child.

Why is it
such categories, such lack of tooth
like the sanded wood, the screws
countersunk
        and hidden.

Floobie
is an Indian name, the occasion
witnessed
as He-Who-Runs-Quick-To-Battle (or)
        The-One-Who-Laughs-All-The-Time
until
he stops doing that.

And we leave that (still wanting it)
  take the names of fathers

        some other relative
grow
into false histories.

The family tree
is bilateral, one trunked, the way
the world seems
outside:
        birds-animals-ourselves,
but inside
a lack of such symmetry;

only the simplest natural things
show us the human face,
transparent, we think we have.

You
placed or rattled something;
It was early morning;
        I was thinking;
I kept sanding,

and *there's* a history: bookcase making
for a corner for you
to work in
your world full of associations—
our move from the City, your achievement,
love, a wish to be otherwise,
books & discovery.

—One
    learns something; that
    always feels at first as if
    one's lost something—
        (that's,
        a little roughly,
        from Shaw).

I don't know.
maybe it's
Things—
not
the possession
of them
        but the living
with them, the subtle absorption until
one moves, and things come out of closets
and we see we don't own them
because they are
not things
but associations,
        nothing
is brute fact. why is it
one loses oneself within them?

It may
be empty is alive. maybe Floobie
is a thing he did
        and does and will do
again, and we too
will do our own names, like
"She-Who-Rattles-Things"
"He-Who-Sands-Wood-In-The-Basement"

I don't
        know. sure it's a hard road.
But while I was below you sanding
you made the sound *floobie,*
you were unaware of? an accident?

who knows? maybe things'll accomplish themselves
with a new regard:

like the sound you made
took me out of myself
    into somebody else's past
and brought me my own present

unexplainable, delicate & certain
Floobie—
    shoobie-do.

Tide Trail

It's not as if
the trail we walked on
took us anywhere: we came
    to the edge of the continent,
waded, and looked around a while
and then were homebound.

    But the trail of sand
became a river as the sea came in,
and there were small fish swimming
trapped, between the boards that marked it
when it was a trail,
and we walked among them
and you caught one in your hand.

Julian—
this is for the tides of our lives of course,
that we can hold them recessional sometimes
and pick and examine their values:
    sandblasted shells and driftwood,
soon enough lost, and probably
more subtle
and beautiful when the tide comes in
to claim them again.

But now I am working too hard at the facts,
and as the trail deepened
it was really
Kathy, wading behind us
    carrying sox and shells and the objects

we might have left there
without her—

     who was overburdened
  and so beautiful
  in her rolled slacks
  in her inquisitiveness
  in her hat
in the sun

that I think I was startled to discover
(though not for the first time)
  the losses and traps in our lives
should we not live them
materially close with another.

I was missing my wife and remembering:
Julian, we too
lived that way once.

Leaving
the trail flooded with fish,
we entered the forest beyond it;
there was some shade there
and a bird singing
  a complex and beautiful song;
we saw, but could not identify.

I was still lonely
but not for the past anymore;
the flats behind us
  were by this time under the sea.
We were now together in the forest.
Kathy was curious about the flowers.

Some Small Movements

The sparrows lift
and flock together in the rain.
Before the rain, after a very stormy night
the sodden tree they sat in
   threw its drops around, but they
were not windswept until it rained again
and they went
somewhere.

Even in the rain
the sparrows seem very dry;
they don't shine, but they do
preen a bit when they have time
when they come back again to the tree.

The sparrows don't have much time; their small
frenetic bodies cook and discover
and quit even the most intricate task
quickly, and they flock together often
and go someplace
it seems only the better to return again
to this tree.

Now it is raining.

The sparrows grow limpid
   and huddle together; the tree
grows weighty from its burden of sparrows and rain
and a few drops slant into my window.
It's as if
there may be something to talk about here.
Then a little sun breaks
and the sparrows flock again.

Come Here

The house sits on the bay's edge, has
large wings we don't see
  in the relatively unassuming nature of
its low-profile presence there.
It's a half mile away.
You're 300
having left yesterday,
gone down to the city for library work
and I'm alone here.

Our cat
was bothering me last night looking for you.
I saw the man who owns the house
the first time this summer
  on his private road, and the white dog he has
for style
running across the moors last night
in a light fog.

It's all right: I painted a little
and bought
  and potted a new plant for you
yesterday. After you'd gone
these things happened
but now it's morning, and I've
little to do.

      No crest of wave, hardly
any part of the bay at all
is visible: it's a foggy day. I sit and think

of fog in another time
and place far less immediate (but
that I think of it.

It was
a snow fog
adrift in the hilly streets, and we
walked in the Arizona snow together—
   night of the first high school dance with her—
She was Mary Lou, her father
was away in Texas
and we
held hands together
in her coat pocket.

   O, that rich passage in agony:
she ragged me
carefully;
I never even got a kiss from her
until the day she left for Texas
and that briefly,
turned
her cheek to me
at the last moment—

   was that love?

Above
The bay at horizon the new clouds
seem to meet the ocean.
The Karok
have it there is a place there
of passage,
      and if

one is pure of heart and chosen
one goes there
and does a life-renewing dance.
   Patipir (the flute boy)
followed her there.
He'd come to desire her house even,
gone a little mad with lust.
He wanted to eat the seaweed dried on its roof.
   He called her "About-the-House Girl," and she'd
always loved the sound of his flute.

I
on the other hand
went down to the Mexican border
   Naco, the Casa Blanca—
The one I loved there
stood in the yard looking at me, saying
"come here"
      (was about 16)
and when I got close to her
she whispered into my ear
"come here":
   I went there
and I forgot Mary Lou,
was cured, as if
that was love.

No crest of wave, no crack of entrance
into those worlds
   and dancing on the earth here will not
settle it: the flood comes on anyway,
is the dull flood of temporary loss, i.e.,
no flood of tears.

This
is not manifestation of love,
but lack of sufficiency
of self, habit & dependency
having lived together
  almost 10 years, lest
that be love.

Well,
the sun's burning the fog off
  revealing the flat surface of sea again,
the bay's curve,
and the practicality of distant
fishing boats,
          and we
  see less than we thought to find there
  when it was foggy.
The house is revealed as a kind of money.
Love is a tricky mystery.

  I read a book;
Thoreau
musing among the primitives on Cape Cod, made
his progress walking along the beach,
would come
a little inland
to find talk and then
return to the sea again. Those

  land stories of dead times,
very quaint) but what he says of the beach edge
seems still true:

"I used to see packs of half-wild dogs haunting
the lonely beach on the south shore
of Staten Island . . .
for the sake of carrion there
cast up."

  Bread on the waters? yes;

deer have more than hunters to fear,
they've
 their own world:
the dogs hunt and harry them until
they become hot and frantic
and spill into the ponds
where they are mired.

And one buck swam
straight into calm Atlantic dusk;
against horizon, a silhouette of antlers gone
into the Karok Gap,
 and the dogs panting on the beach, saying
"come here, come here"—

this, too
was a kind of love.

A book and a few stories, the fog
coming
 like low clouds this time;
a weather like memory:
it seems clear
and then
closes again
 in intensity—until

Dog & Deer, Patipir, the singularity
of each passion
and false loss.

How
do I love thee?
say I am half empty,

see
the strange complexities of weather even
  as if they were here for me.
Let me count the waves,
sit at the beginning of all things future.

Love is a pain in the ass, but is
a strange clearing & mystery.

It's all right,
you'll come here again.

Another Popular Song

"Heart is not the place
to sink or swim; that spear
with feathered dressing on its shaft
you didn't have to stick in me
when tongue would do"—
  I might have said to her.
But I was 14
and fumbling with myself at night
in relatively
chaste thoughts of her; so awkward
when I met with her
I couldn't see she understood
such passion.
  And she left me for another, probably
saw me a little cold and distant
and I was
and still am. She had seemed
like a little bird to me,
  but she was ripe for other things.
She could sing sweetly,
and often did it with others.

Love that is not completed never dies,
and though she is certainly
dead to me in reality,
  she stands up again
in the one who wears
red roses pinned to her hip
when she is sweet 16.

I keep singing to both of them:
you're breaking my heart
slow-poke
earth angel
& other popular songs.

Alvina

For a while now I've had this preoccupation.
I watch even my flowers and trees dying,
and I have not gone
to books for the explanation,
the better to turn from it into some activity.

Caring
for bearberry and rose of Sharon
and a Japanese pine
    there seems to be some question about:
some say it's old age that takes it,
but it has to stand and be sighted
(some green still on the limbs)
until fall comes
in case it was Turpentine Beetle
before we can cut it down.

I'm sure this summer in the parks in cities
you never lived in
are the people your own age sitting
mostly amid the bright bloom of things
who are the ones unpruned and dying there
in the well-kept gardens.

That would be a place to sit, Grandma!
but the carcinoma has got you
down, and a little unfamiliar; at 87
you won't be going out again.

I've a story to tell you: last week
  (in the kind of natural light you like a lot)
I managed
to save two young kingbirds in the nest,
killing the black snake who approached them:
a direct and simple victory—

and that got me
to watching the hundreds of small birds emerging
in this birth season:
I remember
that you like birds and flowers,
and I've been thinking of you a lot.

That was not really a story—
but the point is
that it's things new, inquisitive
and alive
  that have means to bring you to memory.
It was always your mind's tree
I was in love with—
but love lacks
power in this situation.

In the city parks,
though some are wasted of spirit, the people
often outshine the flowers;
like root systems
they've no conventional beauty—

and the dying
Japanese pine
sends up a hundred seedlings;
what I did for the young kingbirds
was meddling:
the snake wound properly
into the tree's anatomy.

And it's August now,
and an early fall is beginning
   to turn the leaves off;
roots hold back
their dispersing of further sustenance,
and a cool wind blows rose petals
around my yard this morning.

It's getting late in the year.
   I can only gather and bring you
these few flowers
the better that you should live a while
with sisters that light the world.

Standard-9, Just One (Some) Of Those Things

The towhee sings in the early rain this morning,
telling me "drink yr tea
drink yr tea,"
   but I've had enough fluid already:
I couldn't handle that.
It's 5:30
and coming on: the windows are misted and closed off;
the rain hats hang with the sun ones
   though a little more prominent (yellow
and bell-clear) because
it's their kind of day.

Way down over the moors
the fog sits
   at bay's edge,
I imagine
planning that fabulous slow flight up here
when the rain gives in a bit
and it cools down
but the forecast says:
rain for two days or more.

How drink in
yr tea, coffee, or even a morning travel whim?
The day is so fully saturated:
it rained all night,
banged on the thin roof and kept me
fitfully half awake
   (though at no loss for a strange dream).
It is not good weather.

Wet trees, flowers, breeze,
what leaves there are
drink up
        and I
even fed the birds a little
dry seed
which is now rain-soaked
but they come anyway
and seem to like it.

Now
the fog comes in on little cat feet—
but that's not true: sudden
name shifts like the fog
changes the shape of things
around us: it takes time to catch up to.

   Gossamer wings of gulls seen
in the high mist and a suspect day moon;
even the lower birds are a little ghostlike
in fog—

and soon
that cloud comes in totally,
it gets dark; only the sharp twitter
of a pair of kingbirds
building a nest in the front yard, now
and then rings.

        *

The residual ritual of the dream then (a little vague)
in which the white youth gang was dressed
only in a kind of loose & scruffy swaddling shorts

& painted
in paisley star clusters
pastel, on one side, from cheek to hip.

   were very thin & almost bald
about 10 of them (aged 9 to 12) dirty
faces & resigned & sad-eyed—
they confronted the black gang, who were
more conventional: black
leather jackets
long hair.

   they wandered aimlessly
in a sandy alley until
at the start of it
somebody rang a weak bell
& one of the white ones threw some object down

   & the two, some-
how chosen ran at each other
linked arms & turned quickly

   & when the smaller (white) was lifted up
the other blacks came in
& struck him (had
kind of leather-covered bats) until
he slid down & then
they kicked & hit him into death
while the other sad
white ones watched it.

And I
   on the backseat of the cab with Sandy
had my tongue in her mouth (the black

back of the driver over the seat)
& I handled her & she
me: we were very urgent
hot & ready at the thought
of painting
   this town we did not really recognize,
were in the wrong neighborhood & this
was the last chance before our deaths:
it was
going to be the white gang's turn soon
& the driver turned & smiled thru glass at us—
"You
should have been aware," he said
   & then I woke up.

     *

How dark it gets
in the morning waking
from such dream travel; how real
     the bitter excitement; even here
each day a sort of adventure:
no mood to be counted on.

I wake often with night fears—
O Sandy,
whose face? whose mouth
   in which my tongue moves? were you
Rachel? were you
that part of my wife, my life
I don't know?

Well—

the bobwhites come at 6
in a gentle rain
on a very windy day
  so overcast it seems
like earlier morning.

They are ground-feeders, and only
very rarely do they disdain
to land on the feeder's boards
and eat a bit—

today
they peck and look
and peck and look again,
the way they have for doing that
when they enter the cut grass of the yard.

They are dreamlike; I mean
they come close
are a little foreign and beautiful;
they stay
and don't stay
for long.

It seems like earlier morning (the dream
holds on) and last night
at 6, it seemed like dawn: the clouds
coming in quick at Coast Guard Beach,
that long
lingering aura before the storm,
the beach empty
and around the seemingly deserted
coast guard station on the hill
a powerful wind.

I heard
her voice over my shoulder as I looked out
turned, and caught her coming
around the building's side
dressed in sweater-covered nightgown
bedroom slippers
long hair;

a black girl
just in she said
to work the summer here, had
locked herself out and the two others
who came down with her
had gone to Provincetown.

And so we had to search a while
to find
an unlatched window
I pushed up and had to hold
and in the other palm
her slippered foot against my knee
and boosted her up and in—

   in the midst of which: her hair
against my face and recognition
of her withered hand,
   strength of the other's grip
against my neck, the ancient
smell and weight and thrust of her,
the torque of muscle
as she rose,
   the certain
closure of the fog

in diminished wind—
until she crossed the sill
and turned
and from that darker space
  smiled out at me.

Every time
we find an open window or trip a lock
there is a kind of exhalation of breath
we did not know
we had in us
as if
the room entered in this
odd but totally proper way
were impossible dream space
    until the window rose
and like a vacuum it began
to accept us in; that there is something
almost clear, but fogged and misty in the way
we lift them over the sill, their haunches
suddenly very close and sweet (jasmine and other
steeped smells) and they
enter while we stay
outside
and turn and smile at us.

I remember the time Paul and I had helped
the female student in
in the same manner, in Aspen; she too
was newly there and had a way
of presenting a pleasant turn of body
in that posture;
we'd smiled across it at each other.

But this time
I smiled across the air
to the outer beach
and picked out a few gulls, windswept
but holding
over the shore's edge.

Now the storm is almost
over here. The two kingbirds return
to gleaning the long grass for food.
    The Indians called them "Little Chief,"
their persistent sense of territory;
they down grackles and other
large birds,
are known to ride on the backs of hawks
who come in too close;

    they are fly-catchers, and that
is a polished art
and a crazy thing to watch: an almost
Walt Disney sense of controlled environment.

Little Chief
takes ownership of the land this morning; it's almost
clear again; the sun tries
to hammer its way through
but it is not yet successful; now and then
a gust throws a few drops of rain against
my window.

I put a jar
for solar tea out on the porch; hardly
any sun comes through at all

and yet by 8
the water starts to get murky.

All these crazy things—

who will I meet next time
Sandy? what power's held over me
to force up
these strange conglomerates? what pained
and desiccated youth gang am I part of?
  how turn the body off from dreaming?

Love is cruel
and strange and a little blind;
  it has a dark underbelly
that cooks and is
too hot not to cool down,

  but it does flair up again
and often and indiscriminate where
it's the body that is concerned:

  whether in the backseats of cars,
in troubled dreams or other
real experiences:

it's one of the only certainties,
therefore unreasonable—
that
may be its craziness: how
bell-clear it gets.

Last night
I couldn't get to sleep at all
after that dream.
It was a waste of time;
  whoever you are
you were on my mind—
but that's fading.

It's 10 now
and the jar is solid and totally
opaque;

  the morning begins to clear up in earnest;
the window loses its tangibility.
I am
suddenly no longer
inside.

It was just one of those things.
The bird says:

        "drink yr tea."

Gulls

The gulls come farther inland when it rains
as if the sea itself
   in its deposits on the land
were there . they drop
and swoop to fish in the longer grass
            then bank
   and rise up puzzled before they hit
then move away
till they get high enough to see
the final demarcation of the land,
then drift
   then hold themselves
in that location.

   /

My heart's in the highlands too sometimes
my body also turned
            to whatever job or pleasure,
   the mind gets lost
dips, and returns again
to you: my Sea of Tranquil Waters.

   /

Always
driving past the dump
we see gulls lining the largest hills,
a string of pearls like wisdom
   halfway between
the garbage and the sea.

Patterns

for William Dalzell

The coffee is turned down low, sputters
and seems to have
  irregular false starts in the kitchen
no rhythm like a metronome.
It'd drive you crazy trying to play
tho a simple kind of song it makes
after 40 beats or so
it's entirely possible there is a pattern
after all.
        The sun
late, because of daylight savings & the energy crisis
nevertheless rises,
  sheets against these dirty windows closing
much of the light out.

I put
grain on the terrace
3 jays come and ignore it, form
the living points of a triangle
spaced out, on the superstructure of the water tower:
blue jays gray with soot.

First day of spring (rain), attend
in the interstices
  a jet trail in high cloud cover.
the jet itself emerges
turns in a bank in its landing pattern
close to a jay's body.
the breasty

clouds clutch the plane between them,
    then melt and fade away.

the coffee fails
& then picks up its beat.

what is revealed?

Oddness, order
and a care for order. the architect
Lightfoot built Claydon House, cut up
and unassuming from the outside
but formal.
and inside, possibly
the most beautifully reasoned staircase
in the 18th century
    (given the Chinese influence
    given the Gothick, spelled with a k)
the carved wood
of the picture frames, the massive
airy shrinelike structure with its empty niche.
    bangles
sputter in the railing's fretwork
at every step,
                    across
inlay
of mother-of-pearl, of ivory.

opulence
at cost of grinding the poor. yes,
but Capability
planted a million seedling trees
for one landscape, that would

not be realized for 4 generations
at a large cost: so

a weird opulence (+) a weirder surety.

Here,
gray jays rise a little and shift
on the black metal. sky is blue now
in the new triangle. jet
is pinned there in its turn
    in the middle of centuries
of technology.
                    the breasty
clouds spread & melt unnaturally,
and beyond that . . .

"But the Solar System!" I protested.
"What the deuce is it to me?" he interrupted impatiently.
"You say that we go round the sun. If we
    went round the moon
it would not make a pennyworth of difference
to me or to my work."
                    That's Sherlock Holmes, a different
kind of capability (end of the 19th century.

Here, back in the 20th again,
    I've left the apartment—
been to a lecture on English Houses—and I'm
walking Lexington Avenue eating macadamia nuts

thinking: earlier, passing
among rich brownstones in the East Sixties
    how the dogs came out in complex patterns

in the mist. plots of grass
squares planted
& small trees cupped in wire
    in the planned concrete, and signs:
CURB YOUR DOG. but they
come out like a symphony:

    an afghan
    shits at a tree's base
    a poodle raises a leg against
somebody's Mercedes. there's a lot of talk
and compliments about breed. a boxer farts discreetly.
they all smell & mark their territories,
a few scowl and yap at encroachment.
there's an evident morning tryst or two.
the owners wear
the skins of dead animals on their backs.
various piles of shit steam in the morning mist.
the street is ripe with plans
    the City Fathers obviously understand.

these are the City Fathers,
who walk their dogs and go
out to their country houses
    and plan formal gardens
and turn the City to ruin.

a street
in London in the 18th century
was a planned affair, a sense of community
shattered here in the 20th:
it's territory these dogs seek
    who live so close together
are driven insane
  by crossed and broken patterns.

in the 19th
it was Pitt Street,
worker tenements under a bridge
in the literal shadow of Westminster Abbey.

"This, Sir, is capable
of becoming a fine landscape":
is how Brown got his name. and made drawings
and planted seeds and saplings, changed
    a river even
into a lake. and now
4 generations later
the whole place has grown
very much the way he drew it: *that's*
Capability,
a lesson to city planners:
    a weird opulence, surely, but
a weirder, realized surety.

The dogs shit
in the morning mist
    which is in my mind now
back on Lexington Avenue with my nuts, heading south
in the afternoon. I find
A maverick arc light / burns in the daylight
at the corner of 61st Street, brighter
even than sun is
    on the bright side
of the avenue.
it helps the sun fire the street.
the rest are dark and blind-eyed
and reasonable,
                until
  clouds cover the street for a while
  and that lone foolish light,
    in place of the solar system,

spots the corner.
when the rest come on at 7
the maverick
'll burn no brighter:
could not pick it out in a crowd.
  the City has it:
  it needs repair, but I
watch it
and think of another maverick:

  "Sherlock Holmes—his limits

1. Knowledge of Literature.—Nil.
2.   "   " Philosophy.—Nil.
3.   "   " Astronomy.—Nil.
4.   Politics.—Feeble.
5.   Botany.—Variable.

. . . .

  Knows nothing of practical gardening.

6. Knowledge of Geology. —Practical, but limited. [but]

. . . .

  He appears to know every detail of every horror
  perpetrated in the century. [and]

. . . .

12. Has a good practical knowledge of British law.

. . . .

                but
certainly came too late for us, e.g.
Ruskin: "Ornament applied to building = Architecture."
or) "If it doesn't naturally move, carve it."

  (although
in Scott's study,
where he wrote *Waverley* & created 'Gothic,' there's
Blake's Canterbury Pilgrims on the wall,
and that's a maverick vortex (-)
a balanced capability.

Jays & plane,
the coffee-sputters,
   and half-mad shitting dogs, begin to fade
I've got
only maverick lights in my head
and a half-gone bag of nuts.
                              I offer
"They're cheaper and better across the street"
to the young woman wanting
macadamia nuts, in the gourmet food shop
in Bloomingdale's.
   who smiles
and says they're for her boss's wife
and cost isn't the issue.

   blond like me, certainly
not from New York either:
   a capable enough midwestern girl,
whose breasts sputter
at every step
bouncing the bangles that she wears

over the tooled fretwork,
and do not fade or melt.
                              the eye
is allowed to stop in cream:
no energy crisis there.
and Sherlock
might have attended that
   tho a little
too analytically. the whole history
of the midwest
   is in her eyes,
where pigs are snuffling still
there, without care for territory.

I want
to *hold* those breasts
but cannot
   make the move fast enough
with her, where

we'd head into the past of
our dumb American surety:

   sock-hops
   the backseats of cars
   fretting with bra's latch
only
to somehow cure
this present pain. the future
is totally out of the question.
   no tangible leavings.
the natural
beauty of the American Countryside, the sad
unplanned ruins of

the elms cut down to allow
houses, that are very pragmatic to go up.
a short view of things
about as far away
   as her breasts are,
and shall remain.

Well,
   she has fine teeth in her smile
like the measured interior of Claydon House,
two cubes forming the great hall
in no way natural.

   She's a maverick tho
as Flo was
and the little pseudo-Chinese dwarflike Buddha God, who
sits
on a pedestal on the floor below
the niche they took him from
to clean it up,
                  and found
he would not fit back again
without they'd possibly
break Lightfoot's carvings up,
who had
Florence Nightingale
   in his foresight,
who lived in Claydon House and put
paintings of dour nurses in those
lovely reasoned frames.

   She gets her nuts
   and leaves, and I

wonder did I turn the coffee off?
is the pot burned?
what am I doing out here?
shopping, I have bought nothing. the clouds
come again
it starts to rain. I imagine

the jays shifting on the slick steel
maintain the shape
    the plane is gone
the damp grain moving unnaturally,
punched & turned by wind,
little grains roll & move:

mavericks all,
but thru that a form attending
hardly worth the effort
defining
    points in a matrix.

a highly confirmed empirical science
mathematics is not
nor geometry
    nor architecture, save
in the use of it
as a surety:

    attend
Lightfoot, Capability, Florence Nightingale (not jays
or 19th-century magpies bringing
all things bright & glittery to prevent
a niche where the eye can rest), the un-
natural beauty of the English Countryside

in which we
  with our limited foresight
cannot dwell:

  opulence (+) surety (-)
the natural beauty of the American Countryside
we have not got
  much left of a quality of regard for (-)
enthusiasm (+)
a fucked-up concern for technology: a most
highly confirmed empirical
science of shortsighted pragmatic nonsense (+)
a total lack of attending (-)
the mad Lightfoot
  and Capability holding
4 generations of seed money.

Like a May Day, it seems
the end of winter's near. I hear
the gray jays'
  identifiable squawks
still in my head,

a paradigm
  that turns them back to blue:
a total, half-assed
locked in the present
American capability,
  a shunt of attention.

I'm home again.
the burnt coffee is close to oil
  (I taste it with my finger.

the jays are gone. the cat
sits at the window watching
the empty tower,
  the fled niche.

In the box of grain
thistle has begun to grow
already, in the turn of one day
  (I attend the few green shoots.

there is no pattern.

But for the cat begins
a certain garden
on which she has designs.

Moot

It is not true that things remain
though, in the ultimate
it is true
      (a useless knowing, but
that it bear us up).

the fact is
different grasses fill each pace,
exchange.
      the birds this year
are not the same as last,

had we but sense
of their generation, could we but mark
  their separate faces
as our own
returns here, yet grows older.

The fact is that the grasses seem
to blow the same,
each bird
turns round familiarly

  lest that we look too close

It is some way our selves remain.
what we left is gone.

Standard-13, I Remember Clifford (From Dick Miller)

The gulls drift and enter
where they have no rights to go: air space
in which the boat-tail grackle
  is pursued by a mockingbird—
the glide and squawk, the beat of heavy
dark wings, until
he's wits enough to land, tuck head in
or quit the territory.
But gulls
have power beyond their age; their attitude,
  as if asleep while flying,
their stiff wings, is of a dignity
if we call that
being untouched by certain trouble.

I enter the bedroom; she's sleeping
under cover this morning—
cool sea breeze
after four days of heat—
  feet and knees together, that posture
we so glibly name, but she's no
fetus: broad territory of the mind's experience
I know nothing of,
and so I don't wake her.

Boats on the breezy bay this morning, drifting
as if a ballroom (domed sky); sails
  may have a way of dancing—
well, that forces it: a march possibly,
the way they lean in progress, tack

back, and turn together, in a certain kind of
timing, but there is no music.

I don't remember
Clifford, but Kenton, the table
at the lively nightclub where you played:
brash of sound
  mellowing into coda at phrase-end,
the two tried to dance to
awkwardly, stepping in quotations for a beat—
too young
to go steady, laura, too young.

    I'm in a dancing mood,
but she is sleeping—
territory
of the mind's experience
like a time in music,
I know nothing of: I don't wake her.

"Could you
play Bud Powell, play Tristano?
  Powell's still alive, isn't he?"
Christ, Poppy,
dead these many years: too many
        old liner notes—she falls
under the table for a quarter;
she goes down for quarters:

that's
in Tristano—
space of associations gathered
in phrases in a language. Poppy's

under his hat's cup like a groupie;
Saul's face is reddening;
the hat holds back the chlorophyll;
her petals wither, and she's
        under the table for a quarter.
I can't find the line yet.
Christ, I should have been a musician.

There's little stutter in the sun this morning,
few clouds attenuate; the smaller birds
fly out of the light
        and sit on limbs in jagged rows,
little zeros of significance,
    obscure notes on the bar.
The boats
have nowhere else to go, and so
turn again in files; close together now,
they're in a *real* dance:
    consideration of partner
in face of danger.

The joke was—
I can only play three tunes:
"over the waves,"
"stars and stripes forever," and
"I remember Clifford"—

    we waited for her to laugh,
who spoke of "Miles" and "Diz"
        and didn't get it, and she went
under the table quickly for a quarter: assertive,
but a shadow of herself to others.
    (Saul's face was reddening), and the trio

came back again
to the melody line—a clarity:
  divorced man with younger woman, insular
desperate and embarrassed,
a little drunk and disheveled—
and they played
I can't get started: Saul and Poppy
did a kind of dancing.

And you are sleeping: territory . . . well,
I've said it— we live in the bass line
or iambic: melody of the mind's experience
of each other, then we wing it.
  You're in a foreign field someplace
I don't know of.
I'm on a beach in California.

The music was portable, the sun
like hot iron in the sky.
  We were turning (on the sand
and the radio)
    searching for something, a station
to agree on. We found
something cool, Christy
  after Kenton, the woman
in the bar song
at the same loose ends. We sucked
lemon ice, and dripped it on the blanket;
our faces were reddening;
    we were squinting.
We married, and went
into a kind of
blind touch-dancing, awkwardly, and soon

lost the rhythm and the tune:
the heat got us down). She remains
   that young fixture in the memory.
Would I
find a similar budding flower were you absent,
a Poppy?); how about you?

The sky darkens as you're waking, stretching;
the boats quit dancing;
   they head for mooring;
the little birds start singing,
familiar,
      as they leave the bar.
The flowers swell and shudder
in anticipation; clouds
attenuate, sun softens, and rain begins
the oldest (saturated) melody: "I remember"—

but Clifford,
brown is the color of my love's eyes,
   not those flesh petals,
black stamens: pupils of opium.

Your breasts are elevated in your stretching;
outside, a summer shower;
you return from that territory—
   dear morning glory—
not a poppy in sight.

And they were
turning on the dance floor; his hat
   held like a tambourine along her thigh.
She was younger than he was,

but not too young. (He would not
    play Bud Powell, play Tristano.)
They went steady in the beat
of *misty, send in the clowns,* and
moon river.

And we, the watchers, moved over
from our shared laughter to those private places:
  starts and endings, doors and gates.
Saul and Poppy
did a kind of dancing, then
turned back to back in bossa nova:
    out of step again,
drunk and disheveled, yet

in territory of their minds' experience
we couldn't know of—
Old Sun (till clouds attenuate) Young Flower.

Shining Hour

The faces of four beautiful women
who sit in chairs, in the living room,
    reading parts of newspapers,
tired after dinner.

Their lips are slightly parted;
their lids are low;
    they seem not to be breathing
under the fabric
of their rough, casual clothing.

A man plays the piano, and enters it;
one turns to him.
    The light is soft in her glasses:
ghost of a chance? shining hour?

Then the eyes of all four are closing,
papers lowered to laps,
        food melting in their stomachs,
those moon curves) under the fabric.

What does a man know, exactly, but money?
Their faces are not lonely;
they are not sad.
        They don't want money:
a circle of pennies
on my desk, *I see your face before me.*

One rises in a while and leaves the room,
and when she returns, she is crying.

What men know is economic
or childish: satisfaction.

She goes to the chair of another,
her own kind to hold her.
   One is newly bewildered,
but the music has her. The men are fools.

Four beautiful women,
in respite in the music that holds them.
I am in love with all of them, and I have money.

The songs are edged with such irony.
This is our quiet evening.

Here's That Rainy Day

Elegance of morning, monument
of silence, where is your language?
It is not
of touching: that is fugitive,
    and if I lift
and fix you
it will be in amber
        (a cat in the amber)
and that's pornography
and is not that language.
    Is it all memory? But,
carefully . . .
these are tales,
and it's the details are the substance
of all there is.

In the memory,
in a chair moved into place for you;
later, you're asleep in the chair:
God knows, there are details—
    traffic of voices to wake you,
radios (my irritations), never
metaphor, but images
and those seen now in the amber.

There's a house then
on the hill seen as the fog
recedes to it;
    raw, after eight years
it seems unfinished, while the larger

weathered one to its right
has settled in;
     in the gap: nothing
but brown and green ground
and the negative space above it, of fog
obscuring the bay.

Memory)
without place or substance,
  you touch my face, my body;
it is an embarrassment
to me—
  touch with no future
or intention, as if
touch itself were the point.
Later,
it is a detail,
it is all there is.

The cat is dead, and still
  she won't go into the ground:
her shadow against my legs,
a whisper of sound at the door,
     (my father's image in the empty chair?),
that other gesture—
forehead against the door frame,
somebody's weeping (can it be me?).

As the world of the dead rises
in its pictures,
  to speak of love
in a time, later, is surely
pornography of the past, and yet

white stockings and *fat black,* the cats
come into the yard boldly;
  new pines stand in their lines
from mother pine: seedlings sent forth
in her dying.

Surely,
it will rain soon and darken
the raw house in the distance,
give it weight and recession
      the cat (as my father did)
go into the earth,
or become ashes.

  Elegance of morning, monument
of a deer seen in the distance
on the damp blacktop;
      I thought it was a dog, but
hesitant and exposed—
it was a deer surely,
a doe, crossing and disappearing
into high growth.

      And I fear
  coming to the subject too quickly, as if
this place were a gathering of subjects:
clouds form over the bay
in soft outlines above the fog,
      blond house and obscured ground; the fog
attenuates and becomes haze;
grass waves bend to the sea.
  The bay's breeze is humid,
though it is still June;

there's a promise of clarity and a sea breeze
after the burn—
then it might rain.

And of the flesh, dear Miriam,
the phallic flesh—
    it comes forth blushing
always, fearing it is a detail
(blush of its brazen youth
  in its wearing body):
wanting a language.

Could wake then to another time,
of promise and resolve—
  her sadly amber flesh that guarded her
from a wanting that she could not name,
in force of pornographic memory
    of yet another time: angelic woman
she could have give in to,
and took his hand
in marriage in her stead.

  Not these comings and goings, not of talk
certainly; possibly of song,
but none from that old school.
What is revealed
now in this new growth (after these rains?),
a quickening
that is a lingering, and does not sprout.
Though *in* the rain:

silent bone spur,
the memory's entablature on the column,

supporting
all gutted monuments. But

    what's this?: a towhee
secretive in the bearberry?
  my hunter, kingbird, on a fragile twig?
and over there—what's that?

2

Your language is hard hit,
so many details,
  honeysuckle, pine:
Japanese & pitch;
beach-plum,
and among named weeds a plastic
coffee cup, the hunter,
rabbiting, dropped—
  rattlebox,
old-field-toad-flax,
ovenbirds & terns
tents at the ends of bare limbs—

it has quickened
and is not that language.

Whine and rhythm of a skill saw in the distance,
nail guns through shingles,
gulls, overhead, through haze;
  then it becomes *fog* again; *candles* dance
obscurely in the new wind—
a false promise of rain?)
though it is cooler now,
and heavier.

Wish to tell you that I love you.
There were comings and goings;
  it faded for a while,
but I was crazy then;

think of anything—
a sudden storm and a longing, a reward
as if it were justice, deer on the blacktop, absence
in the placed chair;

  or think of those wooden fish in *Zona Rosa*;
there were so many . . .
how pick even a dozen
  and be sure of them?—

green cats painted on the walls of their bellies,
tiger tails! Some were a yard long.
Secret,
hints of ritual, saw cuts,
mustaches
  like some women, different
on both sides: smeared with dirt, but
    (lustrous!) even
pink underbellies—twist
of a fish
coming from the mouth
of a fish on the *side* of a fish!
I wanted all
four hundred of them
  (were there more even?).
Just think of it!

I wish to tell you
that I love you:

(she bleached her mustache—
a small brush,
peroxide)

Believe it.

3—ANOTHER SHORE

Did you have the eyes
of other women in your eyes?

It was a brief
sandstorm that touched your lids.

In any case, your blue dress
wet through from swimming—

did you figure
I would release you? was a hunter?

We drank coffee and were
soaked through;

later,
in the west amber room:

plastic cups on a glass table,
another shore.

4

Heart full, of nothing
   I can put my finger on;

the songs have ended but the melodies
     linger, like some standard music:
the tune's memory's fault and love's promise,
the chair empty of its history.

But have passed through
  all those seated and reclining figures,
and they're still half real in the half light
of the mind?);
     they're threadbare
as the worn fabric of headrest,
but they are still warm.

A false promise of rain?
Lilac, when the time is right,
  and saw a *jay* this morning
splitting a *seed*
sunflower
) saw *catbird* and *finch*
at the bath together—
     thoughtless and simple—
and should the rain come
it's no matter: *sparrows* in dark branches
against the wind's slant,
  and all the figures of this world
are perfect.
Here's
less than I wanted to say:

perfect). And so was I!

  I headed up the hill to find her,
holes in my underwear
     and in my faded shirt;

I was thin then and younger.

Gingerbread in the eaves,
a house set in the forest in the mountains
at the end of a long journey.

And she was standing in a shift to greet me,
flowers in her hair, her garment
transparent in door light.
   No inkling, of anything but an entrance,
and she stood aside, out of the light
and waited for me.

   I went into the shaded room,
and she was seated, a box in her lap, a painted
container, a cigar box, inset with hickory.

This was the beginning of the dream only:
   something to do with her hands;
she turned and fingered the box in a shaft of light.
There was a low, cool, fire in the hearth.
It was springtime, but there was a chill in the air.

And how account for the dreaming?
   I was outside looking for the box
and found it under a tree: it was a block of wood,
carved to look like a box, inset with mother-
of-pearl this time, and amber:
a block of wood.

   Then I was somewhere else, in a room
with a woman promising things; the shades were up,
but it was dark in the day in the room

(plastic glasses & an old chair):
outside it was raining.

And what was the meaning of the dream?
dreams have no meaning); there was more of it,
but it's the baggage of narrative that I remember.

The next thing I knew I was holding
a cat encased in a block of amber;
    there was another image in the other side,
but I did not turn it;
        I knew it was not you.

There was the empty chair, the melodies
in the room lingering,
    the tight smile of the dead cat, smile
from another shore, a woman
looking up at me from her knees,
perfect
and really dead). And so was I!

And in a term like memory I saw her reach for me,
her hand clawlike;
    holes in my underwear,
my shirt hung over
the chair's arm now: empty—
        I held
the cat in the block of amber
up and away from her, but she was not moving
toward it, or anything, but me.

Then it was *Maytime*: a tree in flower,
a ruffled bodice and pale cheeks,

a dead one leaning against the trunk,
hint of a smile that drew me
to an afterlife.

She opened her eyes as I approached her
(there was a standard music)
and got up from death to embrace me.
We stood against each other until the blossoms fell—
　　they looked good
on our hair and shoulders
but I think they burned where they landed.

　　That was the whole of it:
dreams have no meaning.
　But I was driven to tell it,
perfect, as I was then
in that drench of blossoms
and those amber-encased figures.

5

A letter from Bob this morning
　(that's a memory)
from Hawaii;
he speaks of colostomy,
says he's joined a special club—
ha, ha—that has its shit together.

The dead speak out in the living,
and there is nothing for it,
no fear strong enough
to abate it:

"I have no major
love in my life at the moment . . .
probably just as well."

Hawaii!
bright sun on the water!
and of an evening
   a bit of amber: a cup
on a glass table, another shore.

6—THAT RAINY DAY

Herring gulls—
a line of fat unstrung pearls
on the dune;
   bits of the line rising
occasionally,
   and then settling,
fragmented waves of the line, lifting
and wheeling;
      a hill, and then another
hill,
and out of sight two more;
then a gradual dip, then dunes again;
then the clear sea—
   all this in the mind (
wash away memory).

A false promise of rain?—no more
   than a dozen or so drops, in irregular
rhythm on the pane, drying
      piecemeal as the sun brightens,
the glass becomes
transparent.

And in the wash of memory's
   dream of pornography and amber,
the cat's in her chair, in your lap
sleeping—
you are both sleeping—
and there is no ground there but detail.

The fog burns off.
The house in the distance
   lightens again and becomes raw;
the workmen are back at the new shingles
of the other house;
I can hear them
calling along the chalk line: rough bird voices
impossible to understand,
   but for the intent of it:
  the sun is out—the shingles
are still cool.

And so was I: that dip
   and flush of love could mark
far less—a cool
column in the shade, a sparrow's
sunny nest in the entablature. Lust
  later.

Off another shore,
fish swim in the shallows, close in:
   their fins cut the water
into turbulence and foam. In the sun
in the wake
they glimmer and have color—
are they painted wood?
are they inset with amber,
      sealed, against all opening?

Grit your teeth): a colostomy,
plastic cups on a glass table,
   a blue dress wet through from swimming,
peroxide . . .
Here's less than I wanted to say:
I meant to tell you that I love you.

And now
over the bright blacktop
      (the deer's vacancy)
a marsh hawk rises,
silver, foreign in his singularity,
hunting (not ever in memory)

It's not going to rain—
but, over there . . .
      what's that?

7

You were standing at the window;
it was early morning. I remember
the light air
   of the space behind you
clear, down to the bay.

No one was awake yet;
it was 6:30—early for you
   but not for me,
for jays, grackles and redwings,
wave of pine candles,
brown thrasher and towhee,
      gulls high and drifting.

The work at the new house was silent,
the shingles even, and shining.

And I remember the air changing—
    invisible waves of the air;
a breeze came up,
and the pine to your side
  shook, and you shifted, or I moved
or the pine moved.

Then a small flock of sparrows gathered
and settled in the pine.
  The tree was behind you now,
and from my angle, the sparrows
    seemed to be sitting on your shoulders
and on your arms when you raised them—
the sun caught them,
      and they shone like amber.

All the birds were singing,
all the trees waving,
  and though it seems strange,
I think I was not dreaming.

The pine candles formed a hat for you.
You were in your best bathrobe;
    it hung, perfect, from the T of you.
I could smell coffee, and honeysuckle, and a mix
of pine pollen.

    The birds lifted
and fluttered, and formed a brief corona
around your head and shoulders.

Your hands were palm up, open, and waiting.

Then the sky darkened,
the windows glazed over;
all the details of the world behind you faded—
we were alone together—
And before I knew it,
it began to rain.